Birds

Denise Ryan

Contents

There are all kinds of birds
and most of them are beautiful!
Let's read about them.

Swans

Swans are large water birds.
Most are white, but some are black.

swan

white feathers

This swan has white feathers
and webbed feet.

large wing

webbed foot

Geese

Geese belong to the same family as swans and ducks.

yellow foot

goose

gray wing feathers

This goose has gray wing feathers
and yellow legs and feet.

Blue Jays

Blue jays have
bright blue feathers.
They eat insects and fruit.

blue jay

The feathers point backward
to make it easier to fly.

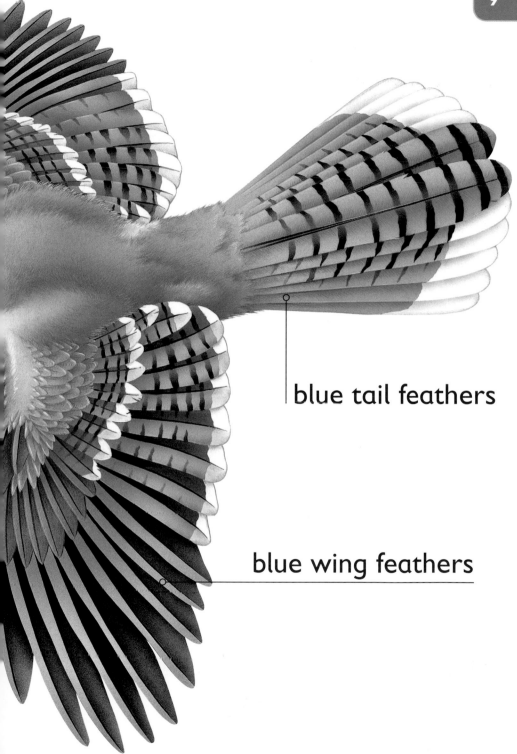

blue tail feathers

blue wing feathers

Toucans

Toucans have enormous bills. They use their bills to pick and crunch up berries and seeds.

yellow bill

toucan

Toucans live in
South America.

Barn Owls

Barn owls have round faces and sharp bills. Their feathers are orange and gray.

barn owl

Barn owls are often hard to see because they come out at night.

round face

sharp bill

Hummingbirds

A hummingbird can flap its wings very fast. It hovers over flowers and feeds on the nectar inside them.

flower

Hummingbirds live in North and Central America.

flapping wing

hummingbird

Penguins

Penguins are unusual birds because they cannot fly. They use their wings like flippers in the water.

Penguins live in the southern part of the world.

wing

penguins

Emus

Emus are very large birds
that cannot fly. They can run
fast and often travel
a long way.

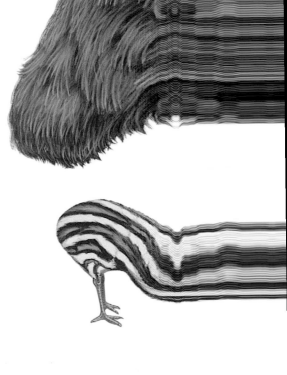

Emus live in Australia.

emu

emu chick

Pelicans

Pelicans are large birds
with enormous, pouched bills,
long wings, and webbed feet.

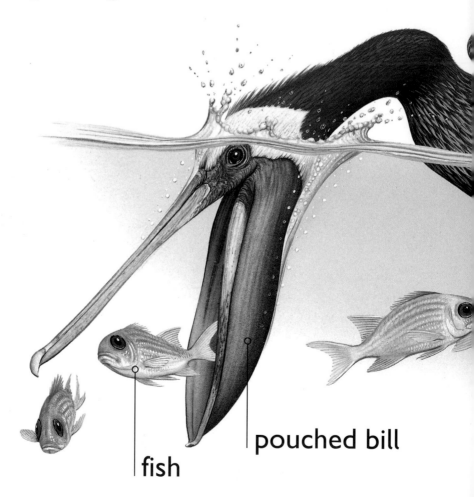

fish

pouched bill

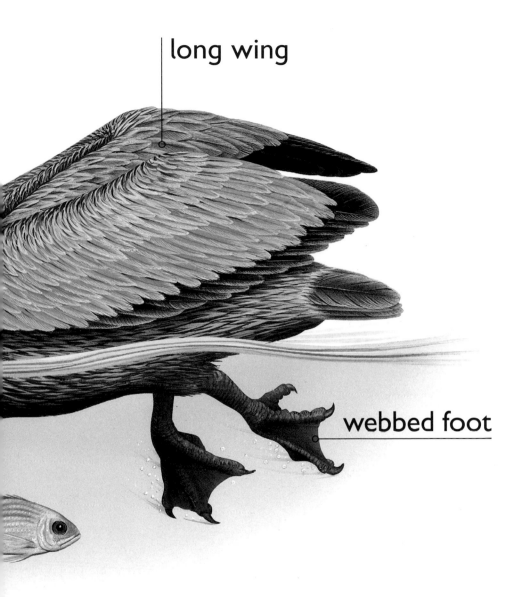

long wing

webbed foot

Pelicans use their bills
to scoop up fish to eat.

Baby Birds

Most birds lay their eggs
in nests. Baby birds grow
in the eggs and then break
out of them.

bird's egg

nest

The mother bird cares for
the eggs and baby birds.

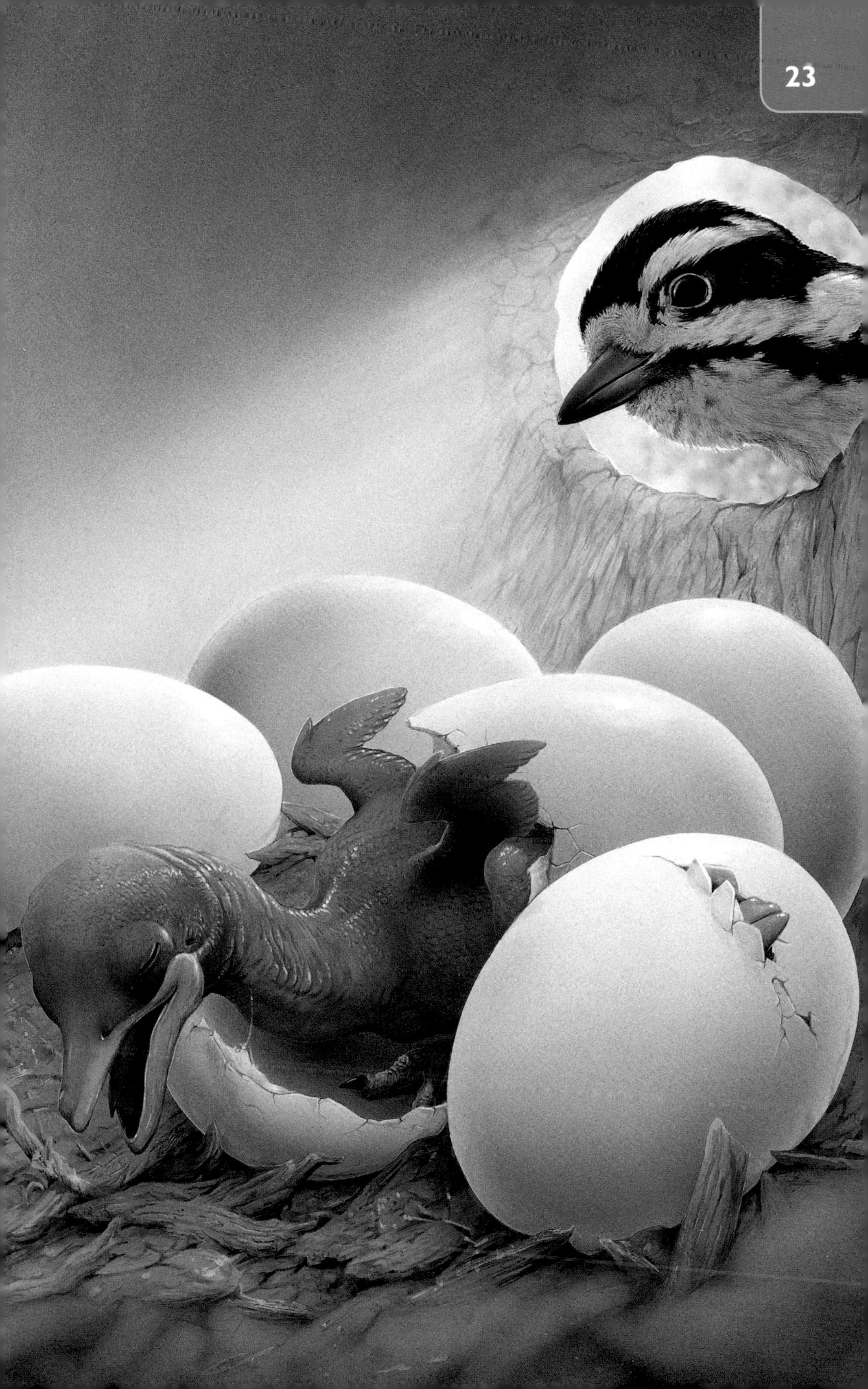

Quiz

Can you match each bird with its name?

blue jay   **hummingbird**

emu   **toucan**